CapCut

Video and Photo Editing Guide

Fast and Easy CapCut Editing Tips

E. Green

TABLE OF CONTENTS

INTRODUCTION

CapCut is a free video editing app created by the same company behind TikTok. Launched globally in April 2020, this user-friendly app quickly captured a significant portion of the video editing market, largely thanks to TikTok's extensive user base. So, how can you use CapCut to create and share videos for fun or other purposes?

We've compiled a comprehensive guide on making great edits with CapCut, including steps from starting a new project and making basic edits to exploring advanced features and exporting your video. This guide also covers tips for optimizing your workflow, utilizing built-in templates, adding music and sound effects, and sharing your creations on social media platforms.

CHAPTER 1

GETTING TO KNOW CAPCUT

What is CapCut?

CapCut is a free, high-quality video editing application developed by ByteDance, the company behind TikTok. Initially launched as ViaMaker, it was rebranded in August 2020 to better align with ByteDance's branding strategy. The app enables users to create and edit videos using a variety of features such as filters, effects, stickers, and music.

Features of CapCut

CapCut is a popular video editing choice due to its features. Here are some key functionalities it offers:

1. **Clip Segmentation**: CapCut enables users to divide clips into smaller segments without losing any video data, making it ideal for creating concise videos or editing longer ones into shorter parts.

2. **Collaborative Tools**: CapCut provides a collaborative feature for real-time project collaboration, beneficial for teams and businesses working on video projects together.

3. **Playback Speed Control**: Users can adjust video playback speed to create slow-motion or fast-motion effects while maintaining high video quality.

4. **Reverse Clips**: CapCut allows clip reversal for creating unique effects, especially useful for crafting entertaining or humorous videos.

5. **Text Editing**: CapCut offers various text editing features like templates, font styles, and bubble effects for adding captions and subtitles to videos.

6. **Audio Enhancement**: CapCut includes a diverse music library, allows importing tracks, and provides sound effects and beat-matching tools.

7. **Chroma Keying**: CapCut features a video background remover tool for extracting main subjects or objects, useful for green screen effects and background removal.

8. **Desktop Editing**: CapCut offers a desktop video editor with advanced features like Script to Video, Auto Reframe, and Auto Captions for professional video creation and streamlined editing.

9. **Template Variety**: CapCut provides a wide selection of templates with color schemes, transitions, animations, and soundtracks for quick and efficient video creation.

10. **User-Friendly Interface**: CapCut boasts an intuitive interface with shortcuts and a streamlined workflow for easy navigation and feature utilization.

11. **Cross-Platform Availability**: CapCut is accessible on both mobile and desktop platforms, allowing users to work on projects seamlessly across devices.

12. **Efficient Performance**: CapCut is optimized to work efficiently on older laptops and handle large 4K video files without frequent software upgrades.

13. **Ad-Free Environment**: CapCut offers an ad-free experience, ensuring uninterrupted focus on video editing tasks.

14. **Video Cropping**: CapCut includes a video cropper for adjusting aspect ratios or frame sizes, beneficial for platform-specific video editing.

15. **Video Trimming**: CapCut features a video trimmer for removing unwanted sections, aiding in creating concise videos or editing longer ones.

16. **Video Merging**: CapCut allows users to merge multiple videos into one, facilitating the creation of longer videos from shorter clips.

17. **Advanced Functionality**: CapCut incorporates advanced features like keyframe animation, curve adjustment, and masking typically found in professional video editing software, catering to both novice and experienced

How to Use CapCut

CapCut is available for download on both iOS and Android platforms via the Apple Store or Google Play Store. Users can start creating videos by importing existing media files or recording new ones directly within the app. After adding media, users can edit them using CapCut's array of tools and features. Once satisfied with their edits, users can export the video in various resolutions, including up to 4K.

Advantages of Using CapCut

CapCut offers several benefits compared to other video editing apps:

- An intuitive interface that is easy to navigate

- Advanced editing tools that allow for the creation of professional-quality videos without prior experience

- A large library of licensed music and sound effects to make videos more engaging

- A variety of filters and effects to enhance visual appeal

- Free to use, making it accessible to a wide range of users

Disadvantages of Using CapCut

- Limited format support, which may not be compatible with some devices or platforms

> In-app purchases for certain advanced features and tools

History and Development of CapCut

CapCut was initially launched in China in 2018 as "Jianying." It quickly became popular due to its user-friendly interface and powerful editing tools. ByteDance acquired the app in 2019 and rebranded it as Viamaker for international markets. CapCut rapidly gained popularity among content creators, influencers, and casual users because of its simplicity, powerful tools, and seamless integration with social media platforms. Over time, it has continued to evolve, adding new features like advanced editing tools, templates, presets, and cloud backup and sync capabilities.

Today, CapCut remains a popular choice for individuals and businesses looking to create professional-quality video content for various purposes, including social media, education, marketing, and personal projects.

System Requirements and Compatibility

CapCut is a mobile app that operates on both iOS and Android devices. Here are the system requirements and compatibility details for each platform:

iOS Compatibility:

> The app requires iOS 11.0 or later.

> It is compatible with iPod Touch, iPad, and iPhone devices.

> Storage needs typically include 200 MB, with additional space required for exported films and project files.

Android Compatibility:

> The app supports Android versions up to and including Android 5.0 (Lollipop).

> It is compatible with various Android tablets and smartphones.

> Storage requirements are similar to iOS, typically needing 200 MB, with more space needed for project files and exported films.

Additional Requirements for CapCut

RAM:

> The app may benefit from a certain level of RAM for optimal performance, although specific requirements are not typically detailed. Devices with higher RAM capacity generally provide better performance.

Internet Connection:

> Although CapCut can be used offline for editing, some features like downloading

music, templates, and effects require an active internet connection.

Software Updates:

➢ Users should ensure their devices are running the latest operating system version to ensure compatibility with the latest CapCut version and access new features and improvements.

Hardware Compatibility:

➢ Some advanced features, such as high-resolution video editing or intensive effects processing, may perform better on devices with more powerful hardware specifications, such as newer processors and graphics capabilities.

Why CapCut is different from other video editing apps

The main differences between CapCut and other video editing apps are:

1. **Ease of Use**: CapCut is known for its intuitive interface, making it accessible to both beginners and experienced users. It has a shorter learning curve compared to other advanced video editing tools, allowing users to start creating content quickly.

2. **Advanced Editing Tools**: CapCut offers a range of sophisticated editing features, such as keyframe animation, curve adjustment, and masking, which are typically found in professional-grade video editing software. It also includes AI-powered tools for tasks like background removal and automatic captioning, streamlining the editing process.

3. **Platform Availability**: CapCut is available on both mobile and desktop platforms, including Windows and macOS, providing users with flexibility in their editing workflow. In contrast, some other apps like InShot are limited to mobile devices only.

4. **Pricing Model**: CapCut is a free-to-use app, making it accessible to a wide range of users. Other apps, such as InShot, offer paid versions with additional features, which may not be suitable for users on a budget.

5. **Social Media Integration**: CapCut is designed with social media content creation in mind. It includes features like instant sharing, caption editing, and compatibility with popular aspect ratios used on platforms like TikTok and Instagram, making it easier to create and distribute content.

6. **Template and Effect Library**: CapCut offers an extensive collection of pre-designed templates and effects, including customizable AI characters and text

templates. This feature set is not always available in other video editing apps, providing users with a wide range of creative options.

7. **Collaboration Capabilities**: While CapCut is well-suited for individual editing needs, Adobe Premiere Pro is better equipped for collaborative projects and complex editing requirements, making it a preferred choice for professional video production teams.

CapCut Templates and Effects

CapCut's templates and effects outshine those of other video editing apps for several reasons:

1. **Extensive Template Library:** CapCut provides a wide array of templates covering various styles, themes, and trends. This broad selection makes it easier for users to find the perfect match for their specific needs and preferences.

2. **Trendy and Visually Appealing:** The templates and effects in CapCut are designed to be visually attractive and aligned with current trends. This helps users create eye-catching videos that engage audiences on popular social media platforms like TikTok.

3. **User-Friendly Design:** CapCut's templates are created with ease of use in mind. Even beginners can produce professional-quality videos with a few clicks,

thanks to the app's intuitive interface and streamlined workflow. This accessibility makes CapCut appealing to users of all skill levels.

4. **Customization Flexibility:** CapCut offers extensive customization options, allowing users to personalize their videos by modifying elements such as text styles, animations, and colors. This flexibility enables the creation of unique and tailored content.

5. **Seamless Integration:** The templates and effects in CapCut are designed to work seamlessly with the app's features and functionalities, ensuring a smooth and efficient editing process and minimizing compatibility issues.

6. **Time-Saving Efficiency:** CapCut's templates come pre-loaded with various elements like keyframes, music beats, filters, and effects, saving users significant time in the editing process. Users can focus on selecting and customizing the right template rather than creating elements from scratch.

7. **Versatile Use Cases:** CapCut's templates cater to a wide range of scenarios, from special events like birthdays and anniversaries to social media content creation, making it a valuable tool for diverse video creation needs.

Things To Note About CapCut Before We Continue

CapCut is an efficient video editing app that is perfect for beginners with no editing experience and content creators looking to quickly produce short videos in bulk. A straightforward editing experience is provided by CapCut, an easy-to-use video editing program with a large template collection and an intuitive UI. Editing short videos or vlogs is made easier with its array of capabilities, which include music, emojis, special effects, filters, and transitions.

CapCut may not be the greatest choice for intricate creative projects or frequent revisions, though, which may limit its applicability for commercial video creation. This is because of its streamlined interface.

This lesson will cover how to add text behind a person in your movies using CapCut's mobile version. CapCut gives consumers the option to edit their films from their desktop PCs or while on the go using its mobile app and internet version. Explore the fascinating possibilities that CapCut provides and discover how to produce eye-catching videos with text overlays that blend in perfectly with your footage.

Understanding CapCut's Advanced Features and Tools

CapCut provides a variety of advanced features and tools that can greatly enhance your video editing capabilities. Below is an overview of its key features:

Timeline

➤ **Arrangement:** Organize and edit video clips.

➤ **Drag and Drop:** Easily rearrange clips.

➤ **Editing:** Trim, split, duplicate, and delete clips directly.

Media Library

➤ **Importing:** Access and import videos, photos, and music from your device.

➤ **Organization:** Organize media files into folders for easy access.

➤ **Search:** Find specific media files using keywords.

Toolbar

➤ **Trim:** Remove unwanted sections from the beginning or end of a clip.

➤ **Split:** Divide a clip into two separate parts at a chosen point.

➤ **Adjust Speed:** Modify the speed of a clip for dramatic or comedic effects.

➤ **Filters:** Enhance your video's visual appearance with various filters.

➤ **Effects:** Add special effects like glitch, blur, and color correction.

- ➢ **Transitions:** Create smooth transitions between clips for seamless flow.

- ➢ **Text:** Insert customizable text with different fonts, colors, and animations.

- ➢ **Stickers:** Decorate your video with stickers and emojis.

- ➢ **Music:** Import background music from your library or use CapCut's built-in options.

- ➢ **Voiceover:** Record narration or voiceovers directly in the app.

- ➢ **Volume:** Adjust the volume levels of clips and background music.

- ➢ **Canvas:** Change the aspect ratio and orientation for different platforms.

- ➢ **Ratio:** Crop the video to fit various aspect ratios like 16:9, 1:1, or 9:16.

- ➢ **Rotate:** Rotate or flip clips for correct orientation or creative effects.

- ➢ **Reverse:** Play clips backward for unique storytelling.

CHAPTER 2

BEGINNING TO USE THE CAPCUT MOBILE APP

Android and iOS Installation

Android Devices Installation:

1. Open the Google Play Store on your Android device.

2. Search for "CapCut" in the search bar.

3. Tap on the "Install" button.

4. Wait for the app to download and install on your device.

For iPhone (iOS) Devices Installation:

1. Open the App Store on your iPhone.

2. Search for "CapCut" using the search function.

3. Tap on the "Get" button.

4. If required, authenticate with your Apple ID (password, Face ID, or Touch ID).

5. Wait for the app to download and install on your iPhone.

See screenshot below:

Android and iPhone (iOS) Setup

1. After opening CapCut, you may be prompted with initial setup steps.

2. Follow the on-screen instructions, which may include:

   ➢ Granting permissions for the app to access media files, camera, and microphone.

   ➢ Signing in or creating an account using your phone number, email, or other supported methods.

➤ Optionally, you can choose to skip the sign-in process and use the app without an account, but some features might be limited.

Main Algorithm

1. **Install and Open CapCut:** Download the CapCut app and launch it on your device.

2. **Create a New Project:** Tap the "New Project" icon to start a new project.

3. **Add Video Clips:** Select one or more video clips and tap "Add."

4. **Begin Editing:** Start editing your video on the CapCut timeline.

5. **Export Video:** Export your video to any format and social platform.

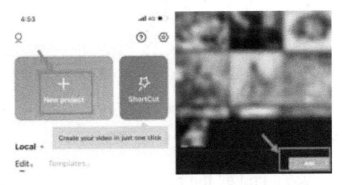

Tips: CapCut automatically saves your project drafts, allowing you to pause and continue editing at any time.

Exploring Capcut Mobile Interface

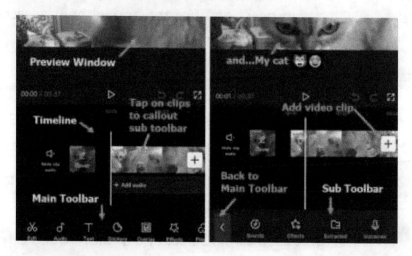

Preview Window:

In this window, you can watch your video playback and interact with your clips directly by pinching, dragging, rotating, and more.

Timeline:

The timeline allows you to arrange and edit various elements such as video, audio, effects, overlays, and text tracks.

Main Toolbar:

Here you'll find all the essential tools required for editing. The Main Toolbar is visible when no clip is chosen on the timeline

Sub Toolbar:

These toolbars are dedicated to specific tracks, and clips on the editing timeline. For example, there are sub-toolbars for video clips, audio, text, and other elements.

CHAPTER 3

HOW TO PERFORM BASIC EDITING IN THE CAPCUT MOBILE APP

Trimming Videos in CapCut

Once videos have been imported into the timeline, use CapCut to cut them as follows:

1. Tap the video file to make it appear with white frames surrounding it.
2. To trim the video, tap and hold the white edge, then drag it.
3. An alternative method to restore clipped pieces is to drag the other end.
4. Adjacent clips will advance to fill in any gaps or create black screens in your project when you edit videos by changing their edges.

You'll need to split the video and remove the portion if you want to take it out of the middle. Instructions are provided below.

Splitting Clips in CapCut

In CapCut, split a video clip by doing the following:

1. 1. Ensure the video clip is selected.
2. Press the Split icon that can be found at the CapCut interface's bottom.

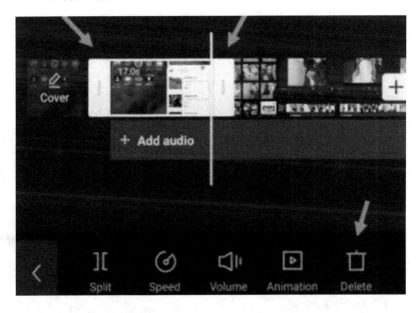

By splitting the video, you can:

- ➤ Insert transitions between segments
- ➤ Eliminate unwanted sections by selecting the split clip and tapping the Delete icon
- ➤ Insert new clips between existing ones

CapCut Video Resizing

With CapCut, you may resize movies to make them more suitable for different social media networks, giving your viewers a better experience.

In CapCut, to resize a video:

1. Choose the video clip that has to be resized.
2. Press the Format icon located at the editor's bottom.
3. Choose a different aspect ratio to fit your needs.

For example, you can change videos from horizontal to vertical for platforms like TikTok by selecting the 9:16 dimension.

Note: Resizing may result in parts of the video being cropped or bounded by black bars. To address this, employ the Canvas feature to refine the video.

CHAPTER 4

USING ADVANCED EDITING FEATURE IN CAPCUT

Adding Canvas in CapCut

1. Select the Canvas icon from the bottom toolbar.

2. Select the Color icon to modify the background color.

3. Utilize the Background feature to incorporate images as the video background.

Advice: If you're editing on a desktop and have low-resolution films, you should use AI video upscaling tools to improve the quality of the clip.

Mirroring Videos in CapCut

With CapCut, mirroring a video horizontally can provide some intriguing effects, such as turning the video horizontally or putting two mirrored videos next to each other.

To horizontally mirror a video:

1. Select the Edit option from the toolbar at the bottom of CapCut after importing the video clips.
2. Click on the Edit menu.
3. To flip the movie horizontally, tap the Mirror tool.

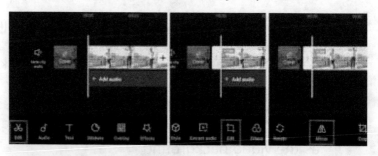

Rotating Videos in CapCut

Rotating videos in CapCut allows you to correct orientations or apply trendy rotation effects with zooming and animation.

In CapCut, you can rotate a movie to alter its orientation:

1. Start a new project, add some video clips, then select Edit. Select the Rotate option.

2. Select the Rotate option

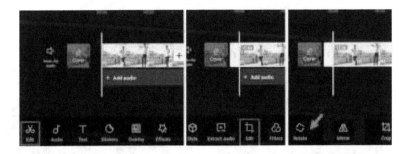

Note: Split the video before using the rotate function if you only want to rotate a portion of it.

Create Motion Effects by Rotating Videos in CapCut with Keyframes

To create a rotating video effect in CapCut:

1. Import your video clips or pictures.

2. Add Keyframes by tapping the icon under the preview window.

3. Move the clip to a new position and add another Keyframe.

4. Use two fingers to pinch and rotate the clip to your desired angle.

5. Repeat steps 3 and 4 to create multiple Keyframes.

6. Play back the video and adjust as needed until you're satisfied with the result.

This process allows you to create a smooth rotating video effect similar to popular trends in CapCut.

Keyframes work by setting the original state of a clip as the first Keyframe. The second Keyframe applies rotation, allowing the video to animate from the original state to the new rotation angle and scale between the two Keyframes, creating the rotation effect.

Using Speed in CapCut:

There are two ways to change the pace of a video with CapCut:

1. Normal Mode: Allows you to adjust the video's speed at a consistent rate, allowing you to set it to 2x, 4x, 8x, etc.

2. Curve Mode: This mode allows for non-linear speed changes, enabling the creation of dramatic speed ramping effects.

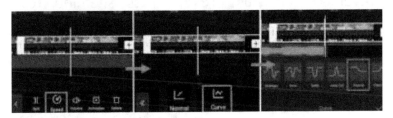

How to Adjust the Speed in CapCut:

Use these procedures to use CapCut's constant speed modifier:

1. Tap the timeline to play the video clip, then click the Speed icon.
2. To change the pace steadily, select the Normal option.
3. Use the slider to adjust the video's speed: drag it to 0.1x or up to 100x.
4. Toggle the Pitch option to select whether to adjust the video speed and audio pitch simultaneously.

You can highlight important moments, such as bullet-time effects, in your slow-motion videos with CapCut's speed modifier.

How to Use CapCut to Reverse a Video

Videos can create interesting effects when they are reversed, such as broken glass seeming restored or shredded paper appearing reassembled.

1. Add the video to your CapCut project
2. Press the video play button.

3. Swipe the bottom toolbar to the right to display the Reverse icon.

4. Reverse the video by clicking the icon

A Clip's Replacement in CapCut

It's easy to change films or images in CapCut while preserving the length and effects of the original clip. In CapCut, replace a video clip with:

1. Tap the video clip that needs to be changed.
2. If required, split the video with the Split tool.
3. Swipe the toolbar until you find the Replace icon.
4. Tap Replace and select the video clip that you want to add.

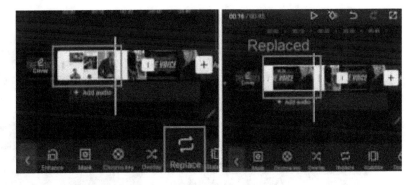

Note: The replaced clip will match the original clip's duration, but you can adjust it as needed.

How to Add Video Transitions in CapCut

Several TikTok transitions are available as one-click templates for use in CapCut Video Editor. These templates allow you to create cool transitions effortlessly, even if you have no editing experience.

To add and Use Transitions in CapCut:

1. Split a lengthy film into two sections, or import multiple videos into a CapCut project.
2. To access the transition panel, click the symbol in the space between the two clips.
3. Try out different transition templates and replay until you find one you like.
4. Take note: To modify or remove transitions, simply tap the symbol again.
5. To change the time of the transition, drag the slider.
6. Press the prohibited symbol to erase any pre-set transition.

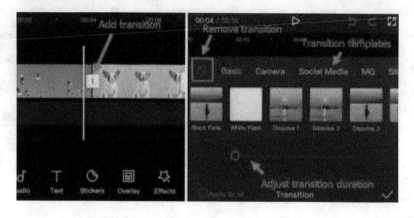

How to Utilize CapCut Overlays

CapCut's overlay tool allows you to superimpose images, text, and movies on top of the main clip to create effects like picture-in-picture, special title effects, and green screen combinations.

Add Overlays in CapCut:

- ➤ Add a photo or video to the project to serve as the feature clip.
- ➤ Select the Overlay toolbar icon. Verify that you haven't chosen the main video clip if you are unable to locate it.
- ➤ From the new window, click the overlay
- ➤ Browse and select a video or picture file to add.

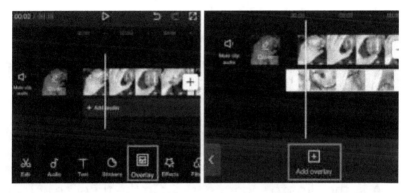

Note: You can repeat the steps if you want to add more overlays to the timeline.

Use CapCut to Edit Overlays:

- ➤ Tap the Overlay track to bring up the editing menu. Similar to the primary clip, you can divide, cut, adjust the volume, and so on.
- ➤ After altering the overlay clip, tap the double arrow icon to access the main timeline again.
- ➤ Click the thumbnail with the droplet shape to return to the Overlay edit panel.

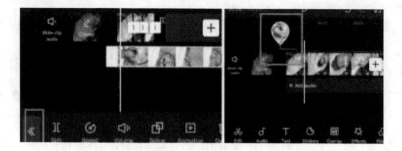

Tips: Your overlay will only appear on black screens with the primary clip visible if it is longer than the original clip. To split or cut the overlay clip, tap it.

You can move the overlay clip on the timeline by tapping and holding it.

How to Make a Split Screen Effect in CapCut by Placing Two Videos Side by Side

Add the clips to separate tracks in the timeline and position them to display two or more at once on the same screen.

Use the crop or split-screen features to select which parts of each clip to show or hide, and to adjust the split-screen shapes as desired.

To begin:

> ➢ Include the primary video in the timeline.
> ➢ Press "Overlay" to include a video overlay.

How to Use CapCut's Green Screen: Chroma Key

CapCut offers a Chroma Key feature for Android users and iOS users to create green screen videos. Before you begin, ensure you have green screen overlays available on your device. You can record a green screen video on your computer and upload it to your device, or you can download green screen images and videos from the internet.

Follow these steps:

Step 1: On your device, open CapCut. To add your videos, tap +New Project. Now, you have the option to choose more than one video.

Step 2: You can now tap on the overlay

Step 3: Next, add the green screen from your phone by tapping on Add Overlay.

Step 4: On the timeline, select the overlayed green screen. Select the revealed Chroma Key option by sliding the bottom tools.

Step 5: Next, drag the circle to choose the color green or any other color you like to be taken out of the background.

Step 6: After choosing Intensity, a slider will appear. To change the intensity, drag the slider from left to right until the chosen color is gone.

Method 2:

Employ CapCut's GreenScreen: Background Eraser

Furthermore, CapCut's backdrop removal ability lets you employ a green screen as well. You may quickly remove the background from your video by using the background removal option. Nevertheless, background removal is limited to Android-powered smartphones. You can go to Method 1 to learn how to create green screen videos in CapCut on iOS devices.

Step 1: Create a new project, and add a video clip

Step 2: Navigate to the bottom and tap overlay.

Step 3: Then tap Add Overlay.

Step 4: After choosing the green screen video in the timeline, scroll the tool from the bottom. Select Remove Background from the tools bar at the bottom.

Step 5: After that, CapCut will instantly take out the green screen background on your movie. You'll notice your green

Tips for Adding Text to CapCut

With CapCut, adding text is simple and quick:

1. When necessary, start a fresh project and import images, audio, and video.
2. Next, tap the text icon.
3. Enter text in any way you want, modifying its font, color, shadow, and other elements.
4. You can adjust the timeline's length by dragging its edge once you've added text.

You can add Effects, and Animation to the Text in addition to the Style tab. You don't require sophisticated editing abilities to work with the settings because they are defaults.

How to Transform Text Transparent Using CapCut

After adding text to the video, you may use CapCut to adjust its transparency to create stunning designs. It might be used, for example, to watermark the videos in CapCut.

1. Select the Text icon, enter your desired text, and then press the confirm button.

2. Drag the Opacity slider in the style tab to change the text and title transparency.

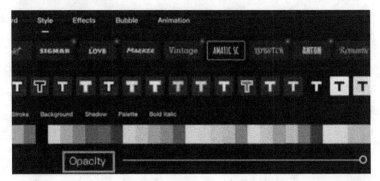

How to Utilize CapCut's Text Tracking Feature

With CapCut's text tracking capability, you may program the text to automatically animate so that it follows a chosen moving object in the film.

1. Tap the Text icon once you have imported the video into the CapCut project.
2. After adding the text to the video, tap on the text segment.
3. To access Tracking, swipe down the toolbar to display it.
4. Drag the arrow to reduce the region to be tracked by the object, then center the anchor over the item's center of motion.
5. To begin auto-tracking, tap the green button for Tracking.

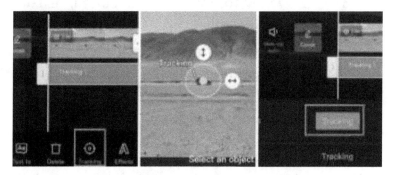

When it's finished, the words will follow the selected object.

Note: By using the graphing tool, you may adjust the tracking motion's easing in and out.

How to Produce the Effect of Text Behind Person

When you combine text editing with other CapCut skills, you may create stylish text effects much like other producers. Placing the text behind the topic is one method to achieve this.

1. As usual, add the text to your video, and export that video clip.
2. Import the video as the primary video track in a new project.
3. Tap overlay to import the unedited, text-free video as the overlay track.
4. After removing the backdrop, make use of the Move background function.

How to Add Audio Feature

CapCut's stock audio library lets you add royalty-free sound effects and background music to your videos, ensuring no copyright issues when posting on social media. Additionally, you can extract music from your favorite videos, but extracted music is suitable for private sharing only. Add your footage to a new project to add audio. On the toolbar, tap the Audio icon.

1. To add your preferred tune, select Sounds to launch the stock library.
2. You can split, trim, or change the pace of the uploaded audio clip by tapping on it.

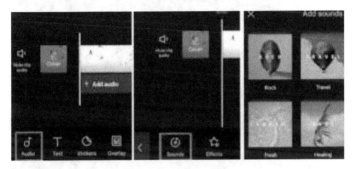

How to Adjust the Audio Level

With the volume option in audio editing, you can mute or make a movie louder.

1. You can adjust the loudness of the background music and ambient sounds in the video by tapping the clip and selecting the Volume icon.

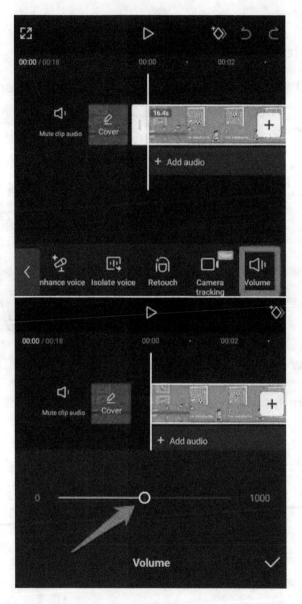

2. Additionally, Tap the video clip and select Extract to split the audio into a separate audio track.

3. Next, you can utilize the Volume feature on the audio clip by tapping on it.

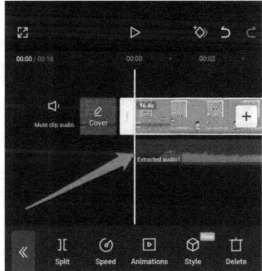

How To Use Auto Caption Feature

To use the Auto Caption feature in CapCut, follow these steps:

1. Start a new project and import your video.
2. Tap the Text icon from the toolbar.
3. Avoid tapping directly on the video to stay in the correct toolbar.
4. Select Auto Captions, found between the Text template and Stickers options.
5. Decide whether to generate auto-captions from the original video sound or a recording.
6. Allow the application to analyze the content and automatically add captions.
7. Play back the video to review the captions. If adjustments are necessary, tap the Batch Edit icon to access the keyboard and make corrections.

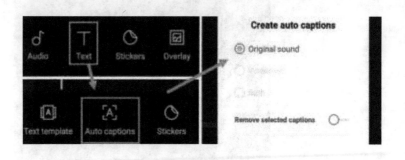

CHAPTER 5

CAPCUT PHOTO EDITING TIPS

Using CapCut Mobile For Photo Editor

CapCut functions as a proficient photo editor, offering a range of robust features for enhancing images. Here is a simplified overview of how CapCut operates as a photo editor:

1. Initiate CapCut: Begin your creative journey by launching the CapCut app on your mobile device, granting access to a plethora of editing tools to enhance your photos.

2. Access the Photo Editor: Locate the "Photo Editor" feature, typically situated in the top left of the interface. This option unveils a collection of editing tools tailored to manifest your creative concepts.

3. Choose an Image: Browse your device's gallery and select the image you want to enhance. CapCut supports various image formats, ensuring compatibility with your preferred pictures.

4. Edit and Personalize: Utilize CapCut's editing tools located below the screen. These tools allow adjustments such as brightness, contrast, saturation, and more. Additionally, apply filters, add text or stickers, and use advanced features like background

51

removal and object manipulation to refine the image to your liking.

5. Export: After finishing your edits, export the edited image to your device's gallery or directly share it with friends to showcase your creative work.

The Mobile photo editor features

Mobile photo editor feature offers a comprehensive suite of features that empower users to elevate their images beyond basic filters. Here's a breakdown of some key capabilities:

Fundamental Editing Tools:

CapCut provides essential editing functions like cropping, resizing, and adjusting the color balance, and lighting. These tools serve as a solid foundation for creating visually appealing images, allowing users to refine their photos with precision.

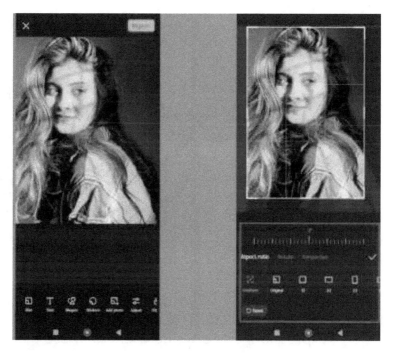

AI-Powered Enhancements:

CapCut leverages advanced AI technology to streamline the editing process. One standout feature is the ability to remove backgrounds with a single tap, opening up endless creative possibilities. Users can seamlessly replace backgrounds, transporting their photos to any desired setting. Additionally, CapCut's AI-driven color adjustment tools automatically optimize the colors in an image, ensuring a polished look without the need for any manual tweaking.

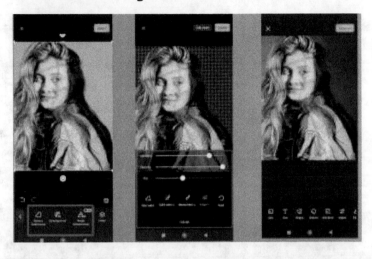

Creative Expression:

CapCut offers a range of tools that foster creative expression, empowering users to infuse their unique style into their photos. The app provides a vast collection of customizable text overlays and stickers,

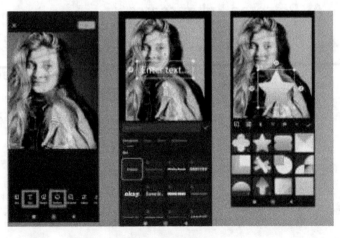

allowing users to add personal touches and convey their message effectively.

Filters and effects further expand creative possibilities, enabling users to transform ordinary photos into artistic masterpieces by adjusting colors, and textures, and applying various artistic styles.

Using the Adjust Features to Fine-tune

Using the adjust feature in CapCut, users can tweak several aspects of their images' appearance, such as brightness and contrast. By assisting users in achieving their intended mood or making up for lighting problems, this application gives their revisions a polished appearance.

By leveraging CapCut's comprehensive set of features, users can elevate their mobile photography and unleash their creative potential, transforming ordinary snapshots into visually stunning works of art.

CHAPTER 6

STEPS TO TROUBLESHOOTING CAPCUT COMMON ERRORS

Troubleshooting CapCut Installation and Crashing Issues

If you encounter difficulties while downloading or installing the latest version of CapCut, consider the following troubleshooting steps:

1. **Verify Your Internet Connection**: Ensure that your device is connected to a stable and reliable internet network. A weak or intermittent connection can hinder the download process.

2. **Check Available Storage Space**: Confirm that your device has sufficient storage capacity to accommodate the CapCut installation. If storage is limited, consider freeing up space by deleting unused files, apps, or media.

3. **Update Your Device's Operating System**: Ensure that your device is running the latest version of its operating system. Outdated software can sometimes cause compatibility issues with newer applications like CapCut.

4. **Download from Trusted Sources**: Always download CapCut from official and verified sources, such as the

Google Play Store for Android devices or the App Store for iOS devices. Avoid using third-party websites or app stores, as they may host modified or malicious versions of the app.

5. **Clear CapCut's Cache and Data**: If you're experiencing crashes or freezing within the app, try clearing its cache and data. This process can help resolve issues caused by corrupted cache files or temporary data.

6. **Use a VPN (if necessary)**: If CapCut is unavailable in your country or region, consider using a virtual private network (VPN) to access the app from a different location. However, ensure that you use a reputable VPN service and follow local laws and regulations.

If CapCut continues to crash or fail to launch, it can be frustrating. Some common causes of these issues include:

1. **Insufficient Device Storage or Memory**: When your device's storage or RAM is nearly full, it can lead to crashes or freezing within CapCut.

2. **Running Multiple Apps Simultaneously**: Using several apps in the background can strain your device's resources, causing CapCut to crash or become unresponsive.

3. **Editing Large Video Files**: Working with high-resolution or lengthy video files can sometimes push

the limits of your device's capabilities, leading to crashes.

4. **Outdated CapCut App or Device**: Using an outdated version of CapCut or an older device with insufficient processing power can contribute to crashing issues.

5. **Old Graphics Card Driver**: On computers, an outdated graphics card driver can cause CapCut to crash or display a black screen.

6. **Other Device Errors**: In some cases, crashes may be caused by underlying issues with your device's software or hardware.

To resolve CapCut crashing issues, try the following methods:

1. **Close Other Running Apps**: Ensure that no other apps are running in the background by closing them. This can help free up resources and prevent crashes.

2. **Restart Your Device**: A simple restart can often resolve temporary glitches or issues that may be causing CapCut to crash.

3. **Free Up Storage Space**: If your device's storage is nearly full, free up space by deleting unused files, apps, or media. This can help improve overall performance and prevent crashes.

4. **Clear CapCut's Cache**: Regularly clearing CapCut's cache data after each project can help maintain smooth functioning and prevent crashes caused by corrupted cache files.

See how:

1. Open Setting

2. Locate Apps

3. Open CapCut

4. Clear Cashe

CHAPTER 7

Future of CapCut

AI-Driven Video Editing

Enhanced Video Editing: CapCut will leverage AI to enhance video editing features, providing users with a seamless and secure experience.

Personalized Content for Businesses

Tailored Marketing: CapCut will assist businesses in creating personalized content for targeted marketing, strengthening customer connections.

Sustainability and Eco-Friendly Messaging

Green Initiatives: CapCut will continue to help businesses highlight their sustainability efforts, focusing on eco-friendly messaging in their content.

Short-Form Video Leadership

Engaging Content: CapCut will maintain its leadership in the short-form video market, offering businesses tools to produce engaging content that resonates with audiences.

By utilizing AI, personalizing content, promoting sustainability, and leading in short-form video, CapCut is set for continued growth and innovation in 2024.

CONCLUSION

This book acts as a thorough manual for CapCut, a video editing application created by the developers of TikTok.

The manual encompasses all aspects of utilizing CapCut, ranging from initiating new projects and executing basic edits to delving into advanced functionalities and exporting videos. It offers practical advice for streamlining your workflow, leveraging pre-set templates, incorporating music and sound effects, and sharing your projects on various social media platforms.

CapCut is especially suitable for novices and content producers aiming to swiftly create short videos. The application boasts an intuitive layout and a diverse array of tools, including emojis, special effects, music, filters, and transitions, making it ideal for editing uncomplicated vlogs or short videos. Nonetheless, its simplified interface may not be conducive to intricate creative endeavors or frequent alterations, thereby limiting its utility for video production.

Centered on the mobile edition of CapCut, this manual also imparts specific editing techniques, like placing text behind individuals, showcasing the exciting potential this software offers for enhancing video production.

INDEX